Chimps

By Cameron Macintosh

Look at the chimps!

Chimps can be very big.

A little chimp can go on
its mum's back.

It clamps on to Mum
with its hands.

Chimps like to chomp on lots of things.

They chomp on nuts and plants.

They chomp on figs, grubs and corn, too!

Chimps can dig with sticks
to get ants to chomp on.

They can crack nuts
with a rock.

This chimp picks ticks
and bugs off its pal.

Then it chomps on the bugs!

Chimps like to have fun.

They like to jump up and up!

Chimps jump from branch to branch.

It's fun to be a chimp!

CHECKING FOR MEANING

1. How can a little chimp move from place to place? *(Literal)*

2. What do chimps like to eat? *(Literal)*

3. What do chimps do to have fun? *(Inferential)*

EXTENDING VOCABULARY

chimps	Look at the word *chimps*. What letter is added to the base word? How does this change the meaning of the word? Add *s* to these words to make a new word meaning *more than one*, e.g. hand, plant, egg, grub, stick, tick.
clamps	What does *clamps* mean in this text? How does a chimp clamp on to its mum?
chomp	What are other words that have a similar meaning to the word *chomp*? E.g. chew, munch, eat.

MOVING BEYOND THE TEXT

1. How are a chimp's hands similar to our hands?
   How is this useful for a chimp?

2. Why does a young chimp ride on its mother's back?

3. Use the photographs to explain where chimps live.

4. Look at the chimps' arms. Why do you think they can jump from branch to branch safely?

SPEED SOUNDS

| ft | mp | nd | nk | st |

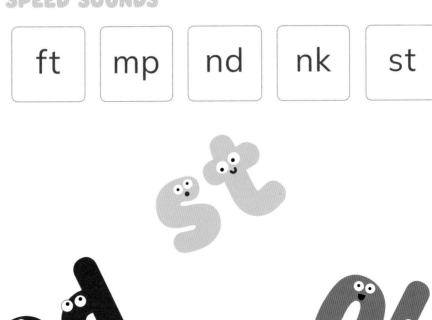

PRACTICE WORDS

Chimps

clamps

chimps

chomp

hands

jump

chimp

and

chomps